Cover Design: Anna Hultgren

For Contact: https://annahultgren.com

Cover Photo: Helio Antonio

For Contact: @helio_antonio on Instagram

ISBN: 978-0-578-34252-8

I Sought the Prophet

a collection of poems

SAMANTHA FISCHER

Table of Contents

Hello, friends.

Welcome to a dream fulfilled.
I am so grateful that you have decided to investigate these pages. Your curiosity is honorable.

In this book, you will find poems that are uncaged and unrestricted. Much of the content you're about to read will inspire you. Plenty of these words will nourish you. Some may even minister to you. However, there are other pieces which may agitate you. Dare I say offend you. This is intentional. Many of us are asleep to the evil that is lurking about in our world. Some of these words are devoted to exposing that. Consider yourself warned.

(That was fun to say.)

With that, narrator Samantha must step back and let these poems have their way.
May you be moved by them. May you be marked by them. May you fall in love again as you read. May you share as you feel stirred. May you brew yourself a cup of tea and take that slow, deep breath you've been avoiding for too long.

Thank you in advance.

Love,

Samantha.

Sweet Love

THE FATHER

you sat on my lap
with trouble on your mind
I softened all my muscles
to coddle you in close,
to pamper you with the affection
you claimed you'd never known.

I'll carry a soft finger to
trace above your ear.
I'll nestle a smooth thumb
to wipe away the tears,
and cradle what's left of either hand
around the base of your skull
to remind you again:
that home is always *here.*

in the meandering of the stratosphere
your once racing pulse will calm,
yet still I'll steer you deeper in
to the depths of peace Himself.
invisible to your eyes, perhaps,
but not invisible to mine.

of flesh and bone and Holy Ghost
I'll curl the barrier. *I am* the post:
the hedge of infinite deflection
that no man or myth or legend
could ever dare wound my baby.

and with effervescent chuckles
I'll coerce your anxiety to yield forevermore

and cause pithy fallacies to fear
for

“shh, now. daddy’s here.”

SIGHT

to see your lover
across a crowded room
invites more than butterflies,
but rather a full-fledged response of
resonance and security.

this gaze is an anchor to the soul
of such mates intertwined —
unbreakable,
unchangeable,
divine.
so much so,
that Cupid could
cast his bow and *still* fail
to conjure up this sort of sign.

to see your lover despite the noise:
this is sight.

DANCING IN 3/4 TIME

waist to waist
we sway side to side
while a waltz of Satie
twirls us by

you've no rush to spin me
or pick up the pace;
this closeness is enough.

old fashioneds and ciders
stain our breath
as soft giggles escape our mouths.

this is better than the movies.
this is better than the fairy tales.
we can't touch the TV screen.
we can't live their reels.

but here in this kitchen
it is better than the books,
dancing
in ¾ time.

MATRIMONY

if he were here
he would set my ribs back
where I've misplaced them.

if he were here
he'd stop the muscles in
my back mid-spasm.

if he were here
he'd ask permission
before he'd kiss me
and swallow my insecurity whole
with a stare of his intent
towards intimacy.

if he were here
things would be different
than they are in this moment
where I sit angry
on the edge of indifference
to the fact that he isn't here *yet.*

if he were here
he'd caress the side of my head
and cup the contours of my sides
before bed.
and in the morning,
despite morning breath,
he would lunge forward in gratefulness
that my lungs did not fail to breathe
and my heart did not fail to beat.

if he were here
I wouldn't write poems in longing
but rather in wonder
at all the things he does
that I never conceived he could,
all the other good things that
imagination had barred from me.

if he were here
he'd be found breathless
at the life that's found in my words
and the love in my eyes.

he'd ponder
how Heaven formed
this creature in front of him
from dust and calcium.
maybe he too will wonder
"why the hell did it take me so long to find her?"
"were the other men asleep?"

no,
they were livid
with anger against the fact
that they couldn't have my body
in train stations and hotel lobbies
and the men in the Beloved
were found asleep,
far more concerned with shallower things.

if he were here
we'd mother and father our friends
who behave like orphans.

we'd find brothers and sisters to guard,
we'd play and enjoy alongside them
and we'd grow all our days.
and pain, though he may come,
will be found victor-less,
dumb
as we conquer him with our love.

if he were here
perhaps it's true that I would write less
but I would be writing from a different sense
a greater sense.
a fonder sense.
a tickled sense.

for a dream fulfilled,
a longing come to pass
truly is a tree of life

if he were here.

FINGERPRINT'S BLUSH

humid air taunts those memories for me
in the absolute best way.
it reminds me of a touch
just below the ear lobe,
of a fingerprint's blush as it scraped
through the surface of my second guessing
and hovered
ever so brilliantly,
near militantly over my carotid.
adorning my pulse.
whispering sweet somethings
of gratitude for my being.
unhurried,
not rushing towards the finale
that your mind is scheming of,
but rather an offering of homecoming:
a refrain of knowing
my wild hopings
now satisfied
by the palm of another.

AUTUMN

it'll soon be fall again
and falling will feel natural,
like warm spice and apple pies.
their restorative symphony
a loud boast
to return to the apple of another's eye.

SILENCE

I'm cherishing the silence

        finding

who he is,
who he isn't,
what he smells like,
what goodness tastes like,
what health looks like.

the senses awakened,
the heart found brazen —
alive and active
in the lack of sound.

cherish the silence in your lover's arms.

LOVER'S VERSE

I once knew
a love so deep
I didn't think
these depths could sink further.
yet here we are;

I am still in love.

LOVERS IN SPRING

cotton-covered fields
and allergy laden air
fail to bother me now,
now that you are here.

now that I know what your scent *feels* like
around me, more so than the pollen that
finds my lips, my hair, my eyes—
scratching tears into my cornea

what I remember instead
are the lips of the lover
I yearned so long for,
thought so long of,
fought so hard for,
strove to find,
but
you came.

oh,
that's all that matters.

MY NOTION

devotion is a declaration
of radical satisfaction,
an arbitration of heart,
a restoration of soul,
remembering the spirit,
reviving the notes
that bring
peace to the ghosts
who have swirled like gas
through our arteries
and atriums,
and our conceptions of lack.
man's strength grows stronger
woman's gait grows confident
at the sound of their names
being called by another
who wholly sees you
for beauty and benevolence alike
regardless of the searing lesions
that have nestled themselves around us.

devotion is a declaration
of radical acceptance.

my notion?
devotion.

Sound Wisdom

BEFORE THE GRAVE

what you will value
at the end of your days
will most likely be warmth
from fleece and from feeling
the intoxicating touch of another —
anyone, truly, that isn't a form of fiction
or an adversary of your time.

and time,
though fleeting,
will not coerce your mind
into pulp and pious predictions
of what ifs and how tos,
and grief, however preemptive
for the lovers of your youth,
should not claim the landscape of your mind.

you'll still crave coffee
though it tastes ever bitter,
and butter with jam on toast
will bring you back to that November
in Paris, and prancing along the
littered sidewalks observing the
skyline.

and should you be so lucky
to reminisce with gladness,
rather than regret,
then her ambience
will not plague you with pain.

for you hadn't forgot to remember
that a poet once told you
to live each day
as if it were good,
as if a Creator had made it just for you,
with your little speck of dust in mind.

STAND BY THESE

we've feared the tidal wave
wondering when Big Brother
would finally rear
his ugly head.

we've traded our freedom for devices
only a few inches long.
for entertainment that strokes
forever and evermore
our ego's eternal shore,
yet a consistent low boil,
a sinister simmer
of acidic anxiety sits
bubbling in our cores.

it should serve as some consolation
to know that they can not
have your character,
your merit,
or your thoughts,
and come gulag or gunshot —
they never will.

Hitler found out
just the same as Mao
that man is seldom victor
in breaking the will of the devout.

but still you ponder
and ever wonder,
"what do we do now?"

at ease, soul!
stand by truth, goodness, and mercy
and recall to mind
for infinites time,
that fear is a foul,
fraudulent liar.

IN THE END

should it all be a lie,
I *still* win.
for I chose to believe
good things all the time.

BLACKMAIL

blackmail is not a fruit of the Spirit,
nor gossip disguised as proceeds of speech,
for the transactions of calloused wounds,
nor bitterness shielded by guards of offense
like the cervix in front of a womb.

I wonder what would happen if we just held our
tongue.

SHAME

shame had built a nasty tent
with holes sprinkled through the top of it.
and the cellophane that made the floor
retained no heat when the winter came.

she tried to host me in her home,
claiming she could keep me safe,
claiming she could assure me warmth
but the space of the interior
could barely hold us both.
she clung to me with a wretched loathe,
yet with the eyes of a pauper
she snuggled close.

I acknowledged that it was gross,
but I let her stay anyways.

it wasn't until the *real* rains came,
those winds, those battering rams of hail,
the rumbling of our earth from the
pitter patter that fell —
that's when I knew I couldn't settle here.

I unzipped the door that had held me captive.
shame did not reach for it,
yet she was not passive.
she exuded with unmatchable force
the image of fear behind a door.
but I left anyways.

her reaction surely showed.

I didn't know that air could be clean.
I didn't know I could brush off the persona of *mean,*
nor that some trees are stronger and greener
than the ones next to them —
but even they don't contemplate their inadequacies;
they grow.

shame is not my home.

THE MILLSTONE

for every pound of shame you lose
you'll lose a pound of fear, too,
and good old standard body weight
may lighten itself of excuse.

the millstone ash upon your neck
sat in between the precipice
of anger, heat, fury, and danger.

it will chisel away
bit by bit,
stone by stone,
'till your body is left
completely whole.

LISTEN TO YOUR BODY

if swelling is a sign of healing
then let it stand to say
that the discomfort you're feeling
may just lead the way.

listen to your body.

LOOK UP

what are you looking for?
in your stares and scrolls
your aches and cravings
in your fight with fiction
what are you *really* searching for?

you crave time at every corner
yet you waste it in your corridors,
your driver's seats
and your restrooms all the same.

you stare down,
a screen frowns at you in return.
have you no life to live up there
like you lived at first?

up from the ground,
up from the waste,
up from the rigamarole of the pace.

up from the glass,
back to the dust —
what you are looking for
has already come!
it's in the wind.
it's in the trees.
it's in the birds.
it's in the leaves.

yet you cannot see
for your eyes are drawn

to a fragile little box
you've cradled since dawn.

have you no mercy on yourself
or consideration for your health?
what you are looking for
can not be found on that thing
you claim connection from.

look up.

FEAR

if you feel the invitation from fear today,
do not give it ear today,
do not give it room to stay.
rather,
run far, *far* away,
and remember —
whatever good promise
your father told you before bed,
that is truth: fear has come to test it.

YOUR VOICE MATTERS

your voice matters,
in process and imperfection
and the incomplete sentences along the way:

hallelujah for grace.

THE NEW GARMENT

to put off all my heaviness
implies that I must
tear the sackcloth from around me
to nestle myself
in comfort
rather than conflict.
to clothe myself in righteousness,
to warm myself in revelation,
to guard myself in gratitude.

a new garment is waiting for you.

WHEN YOU ASK

Wisdom and Her revelations
lay not in a vault or
in a brick of the Smithsonian,
nor in caverns fashioned for wine
or barrels brimming with whiskey.

for there is a well
where a paradigm swells:
the more you ask,
the more you receive.
the more you draw,
the more it fills.
and even as you fall,
the more it spills.

for when you ask, "why?"
Wisdom hears from Her pillars
from those depths of sky,
and communes with brewing minds
to relay the proverbs
of past and of present.

such wisdom is omniscient.

BEAUTY IS PAIN

I remember when I crashed,
full-fledged into talking glass,
its confetti in my hair,
its sting a stare,
a vision of the coming fight
bestowed itself before my eyes.

I watched
as my neck stiffened,
lodged in belts of chiffon.
beauty is pain, right?
wrong.

through tedious years
with tender fingers
I pulled those shards from my curls.
decades later and decades more
I'll learn to embrace the glory of grace —
the messy buns,
the lounging pants,
the teary eyes,
the deep breaths.
make-up free:
honor spilling through my pores
natural and neutral,
honest and holy.

beauty is in the eye of the beholder.

MOLD

to fit a mold that man has made
plastic surgeries call to fame
and fashion's fury main stage.
once you've arrived,
I'm told you'll find love
or so it's been unspoken —
but *said*
that once you acclimate,
once you comply,
once you agree on the dotted line,
that all will be well for you
even on the inside.

lies.

CULTIVATE YOUR CHARACTER

it's more than sitting up straight
            and improving your gait.
                      it's more than stretching when
you're tight;
                                it's communing with your
soul in the dead of night.

a subluxation of the spine is one thing.
interference within your mind is another.

cultivate your character.

ALL THAT IS PRECIOUS

run fast.
      run hard.
            run soon.
far from periwinkles and tarrying tombs
shun the Sheol of yesterday.
and hold fast to your father's gun.
keep it loaded with truth and remembrance.
lest you let it loose from your belt
run fast.
     run hard.
           run soon.
to gather all that is precious to you.

CIRCLE OF LIFE

the circle of life
stays relatively the same.
the chips will fall
wherever they may.
but birth and burden
are not the same.
as un-interchangeable
as night and day.
a scream from lungs demands attention
as a wayward heart commands affection.
the circle of life
is grace in the bay.

may your chips fall kindly,
I pray.

OLD AGE & OLD ADAGES

our hands will grow wrinkly
one day.
yes, they will.
so enjoy them now
as they are not shriveled,
and savor the memories they'll one day carry
when long from now they are.

crave old age and old adages
and do not wish to die young.
our age is to be admired
and the grave should stand
still
as a a place of peace.

crave the wisdom of your elders
and store up proverbs of your own,
to shower on the humble and the forlorn,
to sprinkle far and wide for eternal sweetness.

BEGIN AGAIN

a blank page bathes beside my bed,
begging me to grab a pen
and fill it,
            "please?"
                        it personifies itself to me,
            its lines pulsate with greed.
perhaps the soul cries out the same
to poets and artists and persons alike.
begging that we simply begin.

for the sake of the world
begin.

OPEN YOUR MOUTH

it would sting more if you held your tongue.
when acid flies and songs are sung
to idols and vermin,
their aortas are clenching
in anxious anticipation
for someone
just *one* found righteous to open their mouths
and condemn, full send
injustice.

it burns more to watch the snake of the air
suffocate its victims.

it would sting more if you let the ages pass you by
when your Creator has anointed you
to do,
to speak,
to be all that He's created you to be.

wake up, beloved!
we no longer sleep in apathy.

BRACE YOURSELF

of course
it's easy to organize
around the conflict we do not yet have,
to mobilize the conscience
and ready the psyche
for whatever blow humanity wishes
that it might soon deal on itself
with its own ammunition,
an autoimmune affinity towards its own being —
and we the viewers
scream over and over,
par for the course,
"why are you punching yourself?!"
yet *still* we tense;
we anticipate the burn
of our own fists,
our own sickness,
of our own weapons of war.

but after all this time
you've found as surely as I:
bracing for the blow never really helps.

LONELINESS

the paranoia of loneliness
is a death sentence from invisible matter,
claiming that all is the fault of the self
and the individual is the sole proprietor for growth.
questions unending are vivid in their conclusions,
providing an assassination to the creative girth
of a searching soul,
procuring a vaccine
to all that requests to be known.
anti-viral in its pasture,
causing a fit,
a ceasing of the automatic.
the fever is the symptom,
not the death sentence —
loneliness is not your home.

TRUE NEUTRALITY

this is not an invitation into nothingness;
such a thing does not exist.
numbness, in its fractured frailty
is a far heard cry for something,
for one thing,
for anything,
ah, for intimacy.
the invitation into nothingness
true neutrality cannot exist.
it is not coming
and has not,
nor will it ever,
proceed from Adam's lips.

SUPERSTITION

superstition is not my servant
or my master
or a good steward
of anything I've ever
entrusted it with.

as for mishaps
and mayhem
and answers for tragedies
from psychics
and physics
and astrology alike,
it is not worth your time,
your money,
or your precious energy.

and my two cents
(for all it's worth)
is that
after all is said and done,
we are still in an unseen war.
and perhaps the chaos
and consequence
and couriers of inconvenience
are nothing but the residual effects
of a fallen world
in their desperate attempt
to work out their salvation
or surrender to damnation.
and in the midst of the earth
and her spinning axis,

such little things
are barely collateral damage.

remember:
your blessings always outweigh a curse.

The Interim of Questions

SUFFERING

what does it matter
if the bruises will come?
why pursue joy
at the cost of trust?
why seek after love
to only endure pain?

why encounter hardship
when nihilism, the art of
becoming a shell of a man,
seems a better choice
with less fluctuation,
with less anticipation
between eager good
and evil malice?

what does it matter
if your children will bleed
from tripping on pinecones
and losing baby teeth?
tell me,
what does it matter?

why does the darkness
take the whole of the show,
leaving but moments for the heroes,
whoever they may be,
to sweep in with
bulletproof glee?
"what does it matter?"
you've wondered, so on and so forth

"will it ever?"

it is not a karma covered decree
it is not that yin and yang should fight eternally
suffering cannot carry the weight of such prestige.
even your very questioning shows
that just perhaps this earth on which
you're reading from
was never meant to be your home.

BOUNDARY LINES

the boundary lines have fallen in pleasant places for
me.
have they for you?
or do you wonder
what will eternity do to you?

has Heaven been deemed your portion
with presents for the connected of the Vine?

or have you been granted
a sharp bite from gnashing teeth?
where the question remains to this day:
is the grinding from man or from the devils he'll face?

the Word does not say.
but the consequence beyond the grave
is surely a question you want answered.

what are you willing to lose?

THE MOUNT

parables to me
and crucibles to you,
deciphered by the mean
and welcomed by the prude.

enter?
I do.
I will.
thank you!

into the most censored of views
a harsh, crinkly landscape
where a Jewish man once claimed,
"blessed are the poor in spirit!"
let it settle in the nearness,
the weirdness,
the peculiar nature of it.
the offensiveness of it,
the off-ness of it —
blessed are we?
who are poor and questioning?
yes, you.

Yes.
    You.

FLING

flinging into the mirage of acceptance
I adhered to the rules of religion,
hoping they'd comfort me, father me, even.
into oblivion of self,
oblivion of pain,
it increased them both —
an inflammatory response
to the processing gears
of my aortic tissue.

rest assured:
belonging is simple.
frightful? plentifully so.
delightful? most definitely so.
open arms and honest hearts
cradling my questioning
and disbelief alike,
with trembling limbs
and torrid thoughts:
"too good to be true?"

not.

WISDOM

water wet her limbs,
fire warms her hair,
hope was her hymn,
peace is her share.

the moonlight caught her eyes
as she rose through the air.

if you see the *true* light
then this is my prayer:
will you call me when you get there?

WATCH YOUR MOUTH

do you believe that you lie
justifiably so?
a protective reflex to scurry the ghosts
sat tight in a straddle,
to appease them both —
both angel and demon,
both Heaven and Hell?

you are not the tightrope walker
of underground railroad rumors,
nor an abolitionist of the red light district —
so few can be labeled by such a trope.

do you believe that you lie
justifiably so?

think again.

watch your mouth.

DOES YOUR SHOUT MAKE A DIFFERENCE?

does your shout make the words
feel stronger or smarter or
does the standard in which the diction is raised
go higher or lower,
farther or wider than one's mind could ever gauge?

does your shout make a difference
in public or
private?
for when you yell and one hears
do you mind for their soul
or when you scream in your home,
do you mind for
your own?

tell me:
does your shout make a difference?

QUESTIONS FOR A POLITICAL HARLOT

is that all you have to offer?
after slaughter
and the politicization
of every little thing,
from my cough
to mass shootings,
to the overgrowth of trees?

is all you have to offer
for every ail of society
a blatant stare,
a blank apology,
and a sly smile
which we all knowingly see
as the cameras are turned off.

perhaps you should
put your money where your mouth is
and sew your mouth shut
till you hear the
heartbeat
of the people
you pretend to serve.

ABOLITION

the trafficked cry out in their sleep:
"will no one cry out for me?"
have you not woken
from your own slumber
to realize the plunder of your brothers?
yes, *brothers.*
and sisters and mothers
and nieces and nephews.
when will the fathers we crave
break through?

there's plenty in war rooms
and prayer closets with clutter.
the pregnant and grandmothers
have nestled there for years.
their limbs are tired,
their faith grown pale.
have we no strategy to end this ill?

oh, women of valor,
men of substance,
blessings in advance.

for those who snitch on darkness,
to those who shatter its doors,
to those who valiantly say
no more.

SIN

unreasonable,
            inequitable,
                        political,
                               visceral,
unending, unneeded.
these are better adjectives.
these are better names.

oh Abba,
have you no shame?
so graciously greeting evil done
with mercy and love?
why?
      how?
            what?
for story's sake?
for prodigal sons?

have You seen the breadth of pain
that's been caused by us?
from this flesh and bone?
from these clay cups?

how You have eyes to see and strength to love
amidst our destruction and misery
is mystery enough.

for story's sake.
for prodigal sons.
for one lost sheep.

TO BECOME LOVE

“to become love” —
what would it mean?
for you and I to become a substance
that in and of itself cries intimacy.

to not overlook the man on the street,
drenched in urine and filth on his feet.
to not count the self higher than our brother,
to help our mother, our sister, our father
wherever they lie in society’s eyes.

“to become love” —
what would it be?
for you and me to become beams,
eager to shed our light.

to not brush over the shadow or handkerchief
that can heal bones, sinew, and flesh all the same,
to *not* wrestle with our convictions,
to be like Him who taught us love,
regardless of the variable cost.

“to become love” —
what would it do?
to be step in step with the spirit of Truth,
to be generous when asked, pamper when need be,
to overwhelm anxiety with the sores of His feet.
so blessed are the soles
of those who bring Good News —
for they became love.
will you?

BLUE NO LONGER

blue no longer,
from the curses of tomorrow,
resting in a pool of crimson
though 2,000 years old
still *warm*,
still fresh with redemption.

blue no longer,
who told you to be somber?
have you not heard of an ocean
so rich with love
that color rains
from the wake within?

blue no longer,
blue no more!
through threat of danger
and calls for saviors,
we'll remain
blue no more,
blue no longer.

THE DAYS

each morning the sun rises.
each evening it sets.
tell me, are you God?
can you do that?
have you control over ecosystems?
or authority over the tide?
do you hear the billions of petitions from man
as you sit in the anxious sky?
have you felt the burden of omnipotence?
the caricature of omnipresence?
have you painted sunsets?
breathed stars for fun?
have you sown each seed from inception?
held each man's hand as they died?
each evening the moon rises.
each morning it sets.
remember: you are not God.
you cannot do that.

The Children

EXPECTING

thighs expand
as hearts do,
as do bellies,
and feet
as she grows exponentially
to house this embryo of possibility.
her cells,
his cells,
her wit,
his smile,
all to comprise the body of the being
we've come to know as baby.

A BABY'S CRY

a baby's cry,
whether from colic or hunger,
shouts of undefiled purity.
though born into sin,
she has not yet manifested it.
though it manifests in the air
outside of her home,
it attains time.

she is closer to eternity's throne.
though without a language of her own,
she is smarter than the wisest of scholars,
for she is nearer to the One who knows all the
answers.

a baby's cry,
whether from colic or hunger,
shouts of undefiled purity.
it is that of thunder.

NAPTIME

when they finally give into rest,
it's precious, isn't it?
eyes drifting back and forth,
up and down,
their consciousness turned around —
laying down the world and her troubles
to sit safe in a blanket.

herein lies their bubble
to shield their mind from
conspiracies and controversies alike.
coming whole into their home
of fairytales and fantasies
where the deepest truths hide themselves,
camouflaged in between heroes and villains.

snores pepper their sleeping
while an ever deepening trust
stirs in their bellies,
writing in their brainwaves
holy neuropathways.

COLORING

bring the color
to the bathroom
through the door on the left.

with suds and bubbles
we remember our innocence.

bring the color,
"yes, the violet!"
through the door by the terrace.

with chalk and secrets
we remember our imaginations.

bring the color,
"yes, the brown!"
to the town that is gray.

with smiles we'll remind them
that there's much more to say.

bring the color,
"yes, the yellow!"
to the grief stricken basement.

with pliers and a paintbrush
we'll redeem the light again,
correcting, through color
our attempt
to make things right again.

CARPE DIEM

Peter Pan and pumpkin pie.
the wonder of a summer sky.
the youth have never turned away
the rightness of an autumn day,
for chastity and "pay no mind"
four clover keys
and killing flies:
return to the ways of those closer to the ground
and hindrance —
                    come what may,
we'll find a way
to seize the day.

TOWARDS THE THUNDER

wilderness and wayward wonder,
these children step *towards* the thunder.
shackled with hope, they endeavor
to grope the flickers of light
by candlestick or fireside,
the shimmer of shine by the sea's salt lick.

no fear of future
or tomorrow
or of grave's day.

but rather shackles
of joy
and jumping
and jewels laid by bees.

these are those who accept the mystery.

NOSTALGIA

in the dead of evening I searched for you.
in the woods at twilight, hoping to meet you,
a prayer that you might catch my eye.

I searched behind the kettle's pot
behind the summer's brew,
through the oven's scraps of iron
I sift for proof

that you don't just come and go as you please.
that you're never far away from me.
that you don't come once at Christmas on plates of cookies
nor once upon a withering sunset in fragrant August.

you should come when I ask for you.
you should come when I summon you.

Nostalgia, please.

TO DREAM

to dream is to receive
the wonder of wallowing
in shores undefined,
and stomachs undeterred
by plate after plate
of nourishment forevermore.

to dream is to remember,
are you reckoning once again?
can you feel the weight of feathers
on your supple skin?
do you remember the shift
in the gravity of the air?
flying is only natural,
to care is but a care.

to dream is to revive again
those breathless hearts
and sterile lungs,
that call to God in 4/4,
the nursery's song in 6/8,
and gloat throughout their nights
"awake, awake, o sleeper,"

to dream is to receive
from the child you left in Heaven,
once long forgotten.

RETURNING

before, my dear, once long ago,
before you cherished the primp of prose
before you fought to have your way,
before you thought you ought to seize the now.

before you fought to forget Santa's sleigh,
before you thought that Neverland was fake,
you ought to lift your head a little, to wander, and
gaze a little.

before they stole your blinding light,
before daydreaming was considered blight.
before, my dear, once long ago,
before you matured to status quo.

before is where you must return.
before is where you must go.
before, my dear, is home.

A LETTER TO MY OWN

my daughter, my son:
forget not the days of your youth,
nor trade them in for the lie of adulthood.

hold fast to the evenings and savor the play.
rush out of bed to conquer the day.

my daughter, my son:
forget not the eager rush of truth,
nor trade it in for the lies of vermouth.

hold fast to the fruits and savor the time
drink of living water to rebuke all crimes.

my daughter, my son:
forget not the days of your youth,
nor trade them in for the pride of adulthood.

taste the fruits and forget not the time
it took for the earth to bear such a treat.

hold fast to the evenings and savor the play
and rush out of bed to conquer the day.

GRANDMA MARY

my Grandma is grieved
that my generation has traded in
the truth for a lie.
so she thinks, we place oppression
as a worse offense than murder —
I agree with her.

it makes no sense to us,
no sense to the cells, either.
laid bare on silver trays,
the eyes, the ears, the mouth, the nose.
their lungs won't sing
head, shoulders, knees, and toes.
their heart won't skip a beat
at the first glance of young love.
their bones won't know what it is to break,
nor their muscles what it is to ache.
their lips will never know what it is to be chapped,
nor will they learn the sting of being called fat.
for they never did get the chance to grow plump;
they never did get their full 9 months.
their gestation, their growth —
their opportunity to experience.
their all and all,
their ups and downs,
their rises and falls,
their shows-and-tells.
they will not see the sun rise from our side of Heaven.
they will only eat with Him who is already there.

and somehow, someway

such a scenario is called “merciful.”
reducing them *only* to a clump of cells,
retaining the stance
that modern oppression is too great a weight to bear.
so the unborn receive a free pass
to never experience hell.

but in fact,
in truth,
without trivial dispute
of the short life they knew
inside the hollow womb,
was the oppression of the needle,
the crushing of their skull,
the poison to the heart,
or the crumpling of the whole.

they have tasted hell.
they’ve known it to be sour.

have mercy on us, Lord.

The Prophet

THE UNDERTOW

you weren't ready, were you?
when the water swept you into the undertow.
your breath left your chest, didn't it?
when the arms of the sea claimed you as its own.

you had heard stories of such strength.
you had heard stories of its haughty heights.
you walked the shore
far too many times to count.
you swam into the tame, yet terrific waves,
and experienced a bliss so beautiful you beamed of it.

but you remember, don't you?
when you cried to dive into the depths.
you remember, don't you?
when complacency claimed your creativity.
you remember, don't you?
when you asked to feel Him in every fiber of your
being?

you cried out for the taut, tangible touch of the Triune
Being in technicolor.
you asked, you begged, you waited amongst
frustration.
but be at ease:
Intimacy has heard your cry,
He has yielded Himself to your intentionality.

my beloved, my darling,
it seems that you're quick to blame the undertow.
yet you're the one who yearned to know:

sleeper waves do not differentiate between the beloved and those becoming.
so rest in the unknown of when the undertow is coming.

RETRIBUTION

blood for blood
an eye for an eye
a tooth for a tooth
retribution is a routine for You.

but through toil and trial
the Godhead bowed low,
letting iron pierce His wrists
and split His mangled toes.
and through briar worn sticks
His own flesh conceded
to 39 lashes that would have killed any man.
we, now prized possessions.
us, creation, now blinking at twilight
in whole-found remembrance
asking blissfully
perhaps even ignorantly,
"could anyone really care for us?"
"let alone God, be mindful of us?"

ah, yes!
yes, indeed!
bearing through His own gritted teeth
with untainted divinity
all that was blistered and broken
by these stripes,
killing monotony in every sense of the word.

He gave
blood for blood
a rib for a rib

an eye for an eye
a tooth for a tooth.

His life for our lives.
reproof for reproof.
sin for sin: laid right on Him.
retribution is a routine for You.

hosanna in the highest.

RESURRECTION

verbatim,
point blank,
in the brightness of day.
from the lips of the man
I brought to the grave.
with not a bit of blood
nor a break from bone,
his sinew cried out
as I breathed my refrain,
"Nobility has won.
The old man is done."
the old man is dead.
the new man is come.

so read all about it,
read in the sun.
verbatim
point blank:

THE NEW MAN HAS COME.

THANK YOU

You meant well
when You engulfed me.
a dam of warm body
shielding me
from my own insecurities.

You meant well.
I could feel it in my cells,
from red to white and marrow's genesis
that acceptance,
wholeness
was knocking on my interior's door.

You meant well.
and *that* was what mattered,
what centered the depths of me.
that You've never meant ill towards me.
You've never wished evil on me.

You meant well.
that's what sticks with me
You mean well.
Emmanuel —
presently,
persistently,
eternally.

thank you.

SHEPHERD KING

how can sheep
who know no dialogue
or dialect
know that their Shepherd
is good —
that even in discipline,
even in rebuke,
and even if they run away,
that He *is* good
and has only their best in mind?

perhaps it's the tone of His voice,
the honey under His tongue,
and the immovable smile of grace
plastered on His face.

THE WAR WITHIN

I waste not my energy
for wars waged in vain,
against flesh and bone
and foul days.
                our fathers and mothers
              roll in their graves,
a full rotation for every slain,
for prisoners of war
by evil thoughts.
for captives of old
by their brothers' blood.
a blitzkrieg is needed
for the battle of the spirit.
shall we call on His name?
all matter hears Him say:

Peace. Be still.

NEWS ALERT FROM GOD

news alert:
you
now alert
at the sight of the word:
belt.

not the bellow of angels,
or the screeching of operas,
or the pitter patter of galaxies,
but the bitter hands,
most likely a man's,
groped tightly around the dry hide of a cow,
with a draconian whip,
for any little slip.

"you deserve this,"
                                        you think,
                    or so you thought,
for dispelling lies is a specialty of Mine.

news alert:
you
now alert.
it isn't like Me to hurt you.

LEANING

you'll find me leaning.
not out of humiliation,
not because I've been beaten,
not because I haven't eaten,
but because of the burs that blacken my feet
because of the burrows of grief
for the lovers that denied Him on the Way.

I know how the story ends.
you'll find me leaning in the day
and covered in the night

watch!

my Lover holds me tight.

I SOUGHT THE PROPHET

I sought the prophet
and drew close to His face —
not to hear, but to gaze
an intimate reconciliation
to return to the glow
of the stratosphere that lies within the breadth of His
pores,
that stuns the wildest of predators
and the daintiest of foes.

I sought the prophet
and drew close to His face —
not to receive, but to partake
of the sweetest wines
across universal lines
that threaten the laxest views of the divine,
an unyielding force with the strongest of tones
that confounds the adulterer
and befriends connoisseurs of prose.

I sought the prophet
and drew close to His face —
not to believe, but to find grace
a virtuous journey, a violent trek
through the most colloquial forest in the modern
west,
that grossly convicts and humbly defines
the most dangerous of the dumb
and the wittiest of the wise.

I sought the prophet
and drew close to His face —
He brought me in
and gave me a plate
which disrupts the hierarchy and pummels the saints
the politicians of slander and the ministry of men —
though not in vain and not with pain
He drew me in, close to His face
sought my soul, and kindly proclaimed:

"Man will not rest, until you take My place."

49:16

engraved on the palms of Your hands
are the names of those You choose
and the names of those who
subsequently,
voluntarily,
and with a smile on their face
chose You.

19:16

before tattoos
were ever cautioned
You had a signature
saturated by the pen of God,
written on Your thigh
of all places.

before the seas were created
before You hovered over the deep,
before the Trinity conspired
to breathe life into man,
on Your tender flesh
was a title
that would make all demons
tremble in insatiable fear.

KING OF KINGS
LORD OF LORDS

AUTHOR

Author.
Finisher.
Promise Keeper.

how
do You
in infinity,
within eternity,
plan and plot
my ups and downs
around free will
and free enterprise
and freedom alike,
though wholly mine
has already been predetermined
within Your perfect time.

Author.
Finisher.
Promise Keeper.

clinging to the truth
that even when what is true
doesn't feel true,
I can stagger my way back
to the favorite
of our times —
the fact that you delivered me
through a dream
times two,
at my arrival into the earth

and my arrival into Your kingdom.

Author.
Finisher.
Promise Keeper.
eternally this is You.
from babies in wombs
to dreams in utero
and the awe-filled moments
of *"this just had to be God."*

yes,
that's who You are.
found in my days,
my name,
and my happy place.

Author.
Finisher.
Promise Keeper
Yahweh.

SEARCHING

I searched high and low,
in summer and fall,
in winter and spring,
for anything
                    anything
that might take away this burning hunger within me,
this well of dissatisfaction that clung to me.

the apple could not take it.
the yoke of perfection could not calm it.
the need to be right only exasperated it.
the stares of mankind inflamed it.

but as I strolled in the forest of fervent expectancy
I found a table prepared for me.
with a sign in front:
                    "you who have no money,
                    come, buy and eat!"
with exclamation it welcomed me.

the grapes glistened with pearls.
the meat? roasted and warm.
the lettuce perfect, without blemish.
and all this extravagance — unattended!

a trap must be imminent
but my stomach groaned with tremor.
so I sat.
so I ate.
without utensil or plate
I ate.

first the sweets, then the steak.
it was then when Redemption sang
a premonition of sorts,
the kindest of ghosts:
"*Welcome home.*"

CREATURE'S CHORUS

who has held the earth in His hands?
ah, it's You — this mystery of a Man.
who is Your equal?
perhaps I?
an ant among the atoms of life.
a friend to pleasure, acquainted with grief.
a dreamer, a thinker of finite restriction.

80 years perhaps, 100 at best.
yet —
there are these creatures in Heaven
with eyes all around,
that absorb the majesty
of this One around the throne.
and with infinite wisdom,
from everlasting to everlasting,
all they can shout.
all they can say,
all they care to declare
is
holy
holy
holy.

who is this mystery of a Man?
who is His equal?
who dares question Him?

oh, none other than I!
He delights in my inquisitive eye
so that one day

along with all the saints
I will understand.
I will come to say.
I too will come to shout
as all the cherubim do:
holy
holy
holy
are You.

THE OIL UNSEEN

I write under the anointing of an oil unseen,
under the cover of a wing invisible to me.

I cleave to a concept
held proven by me,
held sure by *"See"*.

I write under the anointing of an oil unseen.
not of puppeteers or puppetry
nor servitude or sorcery.

I write under the cover of a wing invisible to me.
I cleave to a concept
the cosmos can't understand,
that dumbfounds breath and the atoms of sand.

I write under the anointing of an oil unseen.

TIME

surely not behind,
surely not ahead,
surely in the right place
that Time has led.

surely moving forward,
surely in His "Yes,"
surely in the right moment
that Time has said.

surely not behind,
surely not ahead,
surely in the right place —
His Time is correct.

THE FATHER'S TABLE

this is where I'm sitting.
this is where I'm eating.
this is where you'll find me:
at the head of the table.

this is where I'm sitting:
with intimacy as my chair.

this is where I'm eating,
with satisfaction that surpasses
even the most richest of foods
from the most rich of men,
from the most remote of places.
this is where I'm eating:
from satisfaction's plate.

this is where you'll find me:
at the head of an eternal table,
with a robe and a ring placed around me.
what honor is bestowed on persons, let alone
prodigals?
the utensils are set, the placemats arranged,
the lamb freshly slaughtered and a ring of acceptance
nestled tightly around my finger.

this is where I'm sitting.
this is where I'm *staying*.
this is where you'll find me:
at my Father's table.

VENGEANCE

you may try to kill me.
you might.
though know and take note of this:
that even then my blood will cry out in the streets,
first for justice and then for mercy,
what a story it will be:
to have my accusers laid bare before He
who sits on a throne, which carries its own perpetual
Light.

know and take note of this:
Saul was knocked flat off an ass
and onto his own
simply to prove the point of a Ghost
who sits on atoms and undisputed air,
who cares not for murder but for Love's affairs.

know and take note of this:
whoever should wish another harm
one day, once you lay down your arm,
the Man of the Sky will come low in the night
and take care, lest He spare you with mercy.

know and take note of this:
vengeance is the Lord's.

REVELATION'S LEAVES

health is the healing from
Revelation's leaves,
that mere
tender fiber
could banish all disease.
and an oil?
for ailments
that causes suffering to cease.

that such water could flow
and for more than current
be called Living,
beget synonym —
Her name is Life!

which poet calls grief, grim things
the great soil for growth?

the One
who published prose
through such *little* men,
to declare through the work of calloused hands

that health is the healing
which comes from
Revelation's leaves
and that night should forever be day
by the face of a Deity.

THE END OF DAYS

eternity will tell
whether Heaven or hell was
right in its ties.
                    if such language
            of the marriage feast
       with the Lamb
which causes grave offense —
eternity will tell if such a tale was right.

eternity will tell
whether Heaven or hell was
right in its claims.
                         if such language
                     of sacrifice to idols, with intent
           for levitation and gratification
      of pride does not cause great
upset.
eternity will tell if such
a man can be made right.

eternity will tell
at the end of days
whether the book dubbed
Revelation was worthy of its name.

eternity will tell.

EDEN

there were sweet leaves
that when crushed
created a pulp
that the butterflies giggled about
in the garden.

rumor has it that the trees sung
and the wind uplifted, tickling triumph
into every living thing
in the garden.

it stands to say, too,
that the creatures did not maim,
the botanicals did not sting,
the wasps even laughed *(yes, laughed)*
as Adam & Eve waltzed
for the very first time
in the garden.

Elohim Himself strutted around
sans fear of abandonment,
rejoicing in His decision
to choose freedom
rather than slavery,
and beings
rather than robots,
and a conscious will
with constant choices
that could ever choose to reject Him.

yet He was proud of His decision
in the garden.
and contrary to popular belief,
He still is.

www.ingramcontent.com/pod-product-compliance
Ingram Content Group UK Ltd.
Pitfield, Milton Keynes, MK11 3LW, UK
UKHW042003190726
13854UKWH00005B/2140

9 780578 342528